EITEL TIME

The Peregrinzilla Press, Atlanta, Georgia

The Stinehour Press, Lunenburg, Vermont

1995

EITEL TIME
Turnaround Secrets

Charlie Eitel

For my loving wife Cindy
and for our children,
Jennifer, Stephanie and Chuck

ACKNOWLEDGMENTS

For those of you who have never written a book, you probably don't know that the last thing you normally do is write "the acknowledgment." It is not only the last thing. It is the most difficult; at least, it was for me.

I started making a list of my family and friends who I wanted to thank; and I finally gave up on that idea because I decided that I would risk the possibility of inadvertently leaving someone out. The last thing I wanted to do was take the chance of hurting someone's feelings. I finally concluded that there are three people who helped me make this book happen; and without them, I would probably still be thinking about this project instead of being able to say, "It's done!"

So here it is to you, Gordon Whitener, for your inspiration and candor in pushing me to be all that I can be, and to you, Dr. J. Zink, for believing in me, pushing and supporting me in completing the task, and to you, Linda Timms, for your timeless hours of effort and wonderful advice. My heartfelt thanks to each of you!

PREFACE

For the last several years, I've been telling my family and friends that I was going to write a book. Down deep in my heart, I wasn't sure whether I was making this up, or whether I was, in a sense, making a commitment to myself. I guess I set a goal that I would do what is now done.

I am 45 years old. To this point, my life has been exciting and rewarding. The purpose of this little book is to share with you the excitement and rewards of what I call "Eitel" time. I hope that by following the life principles I outline here, you will be able to create your own idle time and have all you require to enjoy it.

Almost every day, a friend or associate comments to my wife, Cindy, and me, "You two really have great kids." Our children, Jennifer, Stephanie and Chuck, are truly remarkable. It is clear that these children are our most important accomplishment. The fact that they turned out to be our most wonderful friends is no accident.

As I think back on how this joyous phenomenon occurred, I realize that raising the children in our long and very happy marriage achieved in the context of powerful business successes has been nothing more than a pervasive series of good life choices. Cindy and I know how to make good choices. Of course, these choices always include a careful consideration of what the results might be if things go wrong. Because, as you must know already, in life, things do go wrong. That is why we all need, as a regular habit, a methodology for making good choices.

I think you will find this book filled with metaphors about "quality of life," both from a business and personal standpoint. These metaphors are all about the process of making good choices, because whether your goal is to turn around a business that is losing money or to increase the quantity of harmonious communication in your family, the most fundamental skill of all is knowing how to make good choices.

In order to understand your personal power in making a good decision, think of a clock that must run "clockwise," and try to focus on your own priorities in life. For example, try to anticipate what it will be like to enter your retirement years.

What will you do? Who will care about you or for you? Who will be in your fan club? From where will come your personal and emotional support? Regardless of age, we all have a future, be it one day or years. How you impact on your own future is worth thinking about today.

I hope you will think about what your priorities are now. By ordering and structuring them, you can design your own timepiece that will be more accurate for you. No one's priority clock works perfectly, but some keep better time than others.

As you read my stories, you will discover what makes my personal priority clock tick. I discovered long ago that an unbalanced clock soon stops ticking.

So each chapter herein (all twelve!) can be seen as an evenhanded way of marking the times of my life. I hope that each hour demarcates for you a method for examining your own priority timepiece.

Because someday I hope you will say to your family, "You know, things have gone so well, I'm going to write a book." Before your time runs out, I hope you do.

Charlie Eitel
Atlanta, Georgia
1995

CONTENTS

INTRODUCTION

In the moving mosaic of faces, ideas, and media that pass through our hectic and often too-hurried lives, every once in a peaceful while, the camera stills and holds the beautifully expressive face of a stunning character — a person you hope gets more time on the stage of the play which is your life.

Such a person for me is Charlie Eitel. I am honored by his request to introduce him and his personal creed to you as I am honored by his friendship.

Even if you do not know Charlie the man, you are about to know Charlie the writer and experience the power of his simple and eloquent convictions about God, life, love and the best way to do business. If you find yourself as charmed as I am by his book, then make a strong effort to meet this man. When you do, you will feel a certain power that flows only from those leaders whose attention, when it is on you, is only on you and nothing else. You will see a look in his eyes that articulates, in ways that words cannot, the fun he is having spending time with you. My, my, you will think, this man loves people.

"If it is a sin to covet honor," Henry V tells us, "then I am the most offending soul alive." Charlie Eitel turns businesses around because he understands that honor, and the choices that travel with it, is the only consistent way to love and lead those who would make the journey with us.

In the past twenty years, it has been my pleasure to meet many of the most powerful, influential leaders of our time. In total candor, I know of none finer, nor more emotionally fit, nor more like Henry V, than Charlie Eitel.

J. Zink, Ph.D.
Manhattan Beach, California

MAKING A
DIFFERENCE

I

I believe the best business organizations in the world are connected by powerful emotions.

GROWING UP I remember spending a lot of time with my grandparents on my father's side. My grandfather, Charles Rush Eitel, was a doctor who was forced to quit practicing medicine at the age of 38 after being stricken with rheumatoid arthritis. What he taught me still guides my life. When I was about 10 years old, he said to me, "There is very little real competition in the world; we are our own greatest competitors."

My grandfather told me that if I could avoid the big mistakes and stay focused, I not only would be successful, but that I could make a big difference in other people's lives. He often talked about setting priorities on one's health, finances, choice of spouse, and treating others equitably. He cited specific examples from his life's store of knowledge. He spoke of talented people who ended up alone. They became, he said, their own enemies.

Early on, I decided that even though I viewed myself as average, I could, in fact, make a difference in my own life by being my own best friend. In this way, I could learn to think through the big decisions in my life and be prepared to forgive myself for making small mistakes along the way. My grandfather, Dr. Eitel, taught me it was okay to make a mistake as long as I learned not to repeat it. This was his greatest gift to me.

Of the thousands of books written on the subject of "Managers vs. Leaders," inevitably the question of whether leaders are born or developed arises. Experts often spend much energy and many pages speculating on what I believe no one knows for dead sure. I honestly don't know whether leaders are born or made, but I do know this: certain people have natural leadership skills. One of my special gifts is recognizing a role model when I see one. If you are not a role model for others, you will not be on my leadership team for very long.

When I was in elementary school, my classmates almost always nominated me for "homeroom president." This amazed me, because back then I was not an academic leader. For some reason, people seemed to think I had leadership skills. At that early age, it never dawned on me what was really happening. Now I realize how few people truly want to lead others. To want to be the leader is to risk failure. I'm convinced that everyone is afraid to fail; it's all a matter of degree.

I do believe that the only way leaders will gain the full measure of self-satisfaction of positively impacting other people's lives is if they are prepared to expose their emotions on a regular basis. By sharing your deep-seated feelings, you give others permission to share what they are feeling. This sharing often bonds you to a secure vision of a mutually beneficial future. This is what I have managed to do well. I have communicated to my team members the vision of an exciting, fun and challenging future.

Much has been written in recent years on the left brain and right brain. It has been observed that people with left brain dominance are more analytical — like engineers, accountants, etc. People with right brain dominance are more creative, artistic, etc. It seems to me that the most effective leaders can function well in both hemispheres. When you are talking to your accountant, you want to be in your left brain. When you are brainstorming with your public relations people, you want to be bouncing around in your right, and you want to have immediate and comfortable access to the side you are not using, in case you need it in a hurry. Like asking "How much will that cost?"

Believing that leadership is more about emotion, I'm convinced that most great leaders tend to live in their right brains. In most cases, dominant right brains marry dominant left brains and vice versa. As the story goes, if two left-brained people are in a relationship, they'll have a boring life and make a lot of money. Two right-brained people will have a grand old time until they're broke.

It seems to me that leaders must learn how to clearly recognize left- and right-brain people, and then help them shore up their non-dominant hemisphere with emotional support and training. I like to see empowered workteams with what I call "brain balance." These teams consider the human side and the bottom line of new ideas and often achieve the maximum in a business deal: happy, motivated employees whose job satisfaction is very high and shareholders who are pleased.

The biggest problem in the business world today is the same as it has always been: poor communication. Ironically, our high speed, computer-aided communication age has failed to allow business people adequate time to examine their own feelings. This illustrates how far we must go to achieve emotional satisfaction in the area of business communication.

I believe the best business organizations in the world are connected by powerful emotions. Getting connected emotionally requires an "event" that is emotional or presents a clear sense of purpose.

On my first Thanksgiving after joining Collins & Aikman (November '87), I decided to have the company give each employee a turkey. This met with criticism from the person who was then my boss, because our division was losing big money. I knew there was not a lot we could do in the way of bonuses that year; but for sure, when the families of our employees joined together for their Thanksgiving dinner, I knew they would think of the importance of Thanksgiving. As the results got better each year, the turkeys got bigger. But those of us who were there will never forget the emotional connection of the Thanksgiving of '87, wondering if we would be able to stay in business. I was determined to give turkeys, not be one.

Human nature is so interesting, because most of us are so competitive on the one hand; yet it's amazing how we tend to root for the underdog on the other. Organizations that are underdogs have a real advantage, if they have leadership. Leaders create a sense of purpose, which is to prove they can survive, win, and even beat the "big guy."

In my business career, which has encompassed leading five companies, I've had one simple mission: to work myself out of a job as soon as possible. I remember during my last few months as President of Collins & Aikman Floor Coverings Division, when I went to work and literally had nothing to do. Our organization became so empowered that everyone knew what to do and how to do it. We were producing record income and having a lot of fun. As a management team, we had mastered working together for a common vision. This "ferocious cooperation" was recognized by all our leaders as creating a good situation for all of us. Bureaucracy and turf defense were minimal. Profit and pride in the team were maximal. I had, in fact, reached a point where my incremental contribution was so small that it was time for me to leave, which I did. My reward is that down deep in my heart, I know that I truly made a difference in the lives of my associates. This was a great period of my life. Both sides of my brain were very pleased, because I had helped create "ferocious cooperation." Creating "ferocious cooperation" is your first emotional task if you are going to be able to afford to give big turkeys.

On November 8, 1993, I made a farewell speech to key associates at Collins & Aikman. It was an emotionally difficult event. I was so proud of what we had accomplished as a team, and we had cultivated many leaders within the group. It was very painful for me to leave this level of love and support. My grandfather was right, of course. We can be our own worst enemies or our own best friends. At Collins & Aikman, I had taught others how to be their own best friends.

What I had done was to get exactly what I wanted by making sure that others got what they wanted. This is the secret to being loved. It is also the secret to financial success.

You see, Grandfather Eitel had a lot to say on both love and money. He said love and money are the only reasons why people do something they would not do naturally.

DOING
WHAT'S
RIGHT

II

I tell our employees we are going to be totally honest and make a lot of money.

I DON'T THINK anyone ever does what's right all the time; however, there are certain individuals who are committed to this mission, regardless of the consequences. These are the ones I want on the team.

At 31 years of age, I became President and Chief Operating Officer of Carriage Carpets. The year prior to my arrival, the company's sales were $6.2 million with a reported operating loss of $234 thousand. Clarence Harris, the founder, was in default of the company's Small Business Administration loan, which was secured by a second mortgage on his home. Needless to say, things looked bleak; however, I was too naive to realize it. What I did know was that I had an opportunity of a lifetime. Clarence had agreed to sell me 12% of the company. This turned out to be a difficult feat in view of the fact he didn't have the stock to sell. After a two-year redemption procedure of his original shareholders, I finally got my stock.

A man I will call "Jackson" owned approximately one-third of the company. He filled the position of Vice President of Manufacturing and reported to me. At that time, Carriage Carpet's key market segments were mobile homes and recreational vehicles. I learned through history that Jackson had a habit of substituting raw carpet materials on a regular basis, as they became available at a lower cost. Early on in my tenure at Carriage, I made up my mind that we were going to be totally honest with our customers. I believed this strategy would be a key to gaining market share. We were going to do everything right the first time. Grandfather Eitel taught me this: total integrity. But total integrity was a unique concept to the carpet industry at that time. Our markets were extremely price sensitive, and Carriage was known for being higher priced than competition.

Early on, I told Jackson that we were going to set tight standards in materials; and under no circumstances, would we alter a specification. Then the day came when I got a call from one of our sales people in the field, notifying me that we had shipped several thousand yards of streaked carpet. After investigating the facts, I learned that "Jackson had done it again." He had substituted a less expensive yarn to increase our profit margin. Later that day, Jackson and I reviewed the balance of the product run, which was in our warehouse in Calhoun, Georgia. This carpet was also defective. I told Jackson to grade all the material as seconds. I said, "We are prepared to compete on price — not through price." He said, "You are crazy," and went straight to Clarence. Honorably, Clarence reminded Jackson that he worked for me; and that I was running the company. Jackson said if that was the case, he wanted to sell his stock. The company's book value was worth $1.8 million; therefore, Jackson's share was about $600 thousand. The next day Clarence offered him $700 thousand and they cut a deal. Three years later, we took Carriage public with sales of $75 million. Jackson's one-third would have been worth close to $10 million.

In 1981, I'm sure it was difficult for Jackson to understand how a 31-year-old kid could know more than he did about manufacturing. The reality of it is, I didn't, but I did know that to build Carriage, we needed total integrity. As Grandfather Eitel said, "Do it right the first time or don't do it."

To this day, I tell our employees, "We're going to be totally honest and make a lot of money." When I left Carriage in 1986, we were the top-performing textile company in every published performance ratio.

Another way to consider the Carriage story, in perspective, is to look at the simple but profound work of Lou Holtz, who is the coach of Notre Dame's football team. A few years ago, I saw a video he did entitled, "Do Right." Lou simply asks three questions of his players and coaches:

1. *Can I trust you?*
2. *Are you committed?*
3. *Do you care about me?*

These three questions are the foundation of all human relationships. All business relationships that last must have trust, commitment and caring as their core values. Otherwise, businessmen and women are con artists who run bait and switch games.

In the middle of the dramatic turnaround of Collins & Aikman Floorcoverings, I got a call that I will never forget. The co-owners of Collins & Aikman, Wasserstein Perella and

Blackstone, had decided to sell the Floorcoverings Division. This move really did not surprise me. The co-owners had neither vision nor basic understanding of our business. They seemed not to care about the people who worked for them. Nor did they believe what I was telling them was true. I had told them that the business was about to turn very profitable and selling it would be a terrible mistake. I also told them if they insisted on a sale, I wanted to be a buyer. I had been promised this opportunity by my former boss, Sandy Sigoloff, who had since left the company.

When Randy Weisenburger of Wasserstein Perella showed up in Dalton, Georgia, to make the big announcement to our management team, I made a decision that none of us will ever forget. After being told I could not be a buyer, I excused myself and four top managers from the meeting to the hallway. Here's what I said:

> *"Do you trust me?"*
> *"Are you committed?"*
> *"Do you care about me?"*

We all answered, "Yes" to each other on all three questions, and then I said, "Are each of you individually prepared to put your job on the line?" They all said, "Yes."

We went back into the room and I announced to Randy Weisenburger that we were all quitting our current jobs in order to be buyers. Randy turned white, excused himself, then returned one hour later to say they had changed their minds, and that our team, in fact, could be buyers in this one, very unique situation.

The exercise they went through in trying to sell the Floorcoverings Division was a waste of time. The only real offer they got was from our team. They never did sell the division; and within two years, the value of the business had more than doubled.

In life, we often find ourselves in situations where we clearly know what's right, but we simply don't have the guts to "step up to the plate" and make hard decisions. No one does what's right all the time, but I believe if we continually think about the price for a bad choice, we will make better choices.

I was proud of my team that day in Dalton. We stood up for what we believed in because we had trust, commitment and caring for each other. We were prepared to face disaster together and because we were, we achieved a great moral victory for ourselves and each other.

This team bonding is the essence of "ferocious cooperation." Believe me, there is no stronger force in nature! Sociologists who study warfare tell us that trust, commitment and caring are the forces that forge the foxhole friendships that last a lifetime. You find out who your real friends are in a hurry when the fast bullets fly. And you never forget them.

That day in Dalton illustrates perfectly the attitude I have tried to instill in the companies I have led. I do this by matching my words with my deeds and being willing to go to the wall with and for my team.

TRUSTING
INTENTIONS

III

There is enough competition in the world without creating it within our own companies.

MANY BOOKS HAVE been published on the subject of communication. They all, invariably, illustrate how miscommunication leads to doubt, creates stress and often results in emotional pain. I have always tried to receive information from a positive, optimistic view. I admit that this approach is often risky. My starting point is with the belief that people, in fact, are trying to do what's right. By the same token, if I ever determine someone is a perpetual politician who spends most of his or her time manipulating others, they usually don't make it with me. There is enough competition in this world without creating it within our own companies. The important point here is to start by giving people the benefit of the doubt and, in fact, assume they do have "trusting intentions." We're all different, but we're all okay.

Earlier, I mentioned helping people get what they want. Here is an example. When I was president of Collins & Aikman, we started a GED (General Equivalency Diploma) program on company time. We encouraged our associates to go to school for four hours a week. They were paid as if they worked for the company for those four hours. We paid teachers and tutors to deliver the program. We even paid for the books. My associate and close friend, Gordon Whitener, who is now President of the Americas Division of Interface Floorcoverings Group, helped mastermind this idea. The idea made sense to us because it is the right thing to do. It has also made a significant impact on the educational system in America.

At the time we started the program, I didn't think the idea was that original. However, *The Wall Street Journal* and "NBC Nightly News" did. They both came to Dalton, Georgia, to film and write about our employees going to school on company time. I was asked by "NBC Nightly News" reporters how I justified such an expense. They wanted to know how we would get our money back. Like typical journalists, they failed to trust the intentions of our employees and asked me, "How will you feel if you invest a lot of money in one of your employee's education and he or she simply quits?" My response was, "My job is to create an environment where people will want to stay." More specifically, I have trusting intentions that people want to better themselves. My job as a leader is to create environments where they can grow and flourish. If at some point, they want to grow further and our company can't provide new opportunities, so be it; everyone still wins.

Leaving Collins & Aikman was traumatic because of the relationships that I had with the people — not just management, but rather the people on the "shop floor" as well. The name Yanett Hackney may not be familiar to most of the readers of this book, but I can assure you that I will never forget Yanett as long as I live. She is a long-term employee of Collins & Aikman who works in the yarn-beaming area of the tufting plant. She, along with more than 100 associates, graduated with her GED on company time. A few hours before my departure, Yanett came into my office (unannounced, which people often did) with a gift, actually with several gifts.

She began the conversation by holding up her paycheck and saying, "This is the most money I have ever made in one year. Thank you." That was gift number one. I thought this was quite interesting because the Floorcoverings Division of Collins & Aikman was in the process of posting a record income year as well. The next thing Yanett did was present me with a silver dollar, encased in cardboard and plastic, implying it was very special. In fact, it was special because the date on it, 1939, was the year she was born. She explained that her mother had given it to her as a small child and told her to rub it every day for good luck. She handed me the coin with one hand and proudly displayed her company inscribed class ring on the other. I'll never forget what she said, "I love you Charlie and thanks for all you've done for me. Please rub this coin every day for good luck and come back and get us."

This coin is one of the most meaningful gifts anyone has ever given me. My thoughts of Yanett and her sincerity in sharing her gifts with me bring tears of happiness. You know, I never really knew her as a person until that day. But I am warmed by the thought that I made a difference in her life.

You see, leadership is not about money, prestige, and power. It isn't about limousines and private jets. Gordon

Gecko in the movie, "Wall Street," was dead wrong when he said "Greed is good."

In the movie, "A Few Good Men," the Marine had it right when he was convicted on only one count. He said, "Guilty? Why are we guilty?" The other convicted Marine answered him, "Because we forgot the duty of the strong is to protect the weak, not exploit them."

We live in an age when cultivating relationships with our customer-clients is viewed by most as essential to long-term business growth.

Until business leaders recognize that their own employees are their first customer-clients, and that these employees will treat the cash-paying customer-clients exactly as they themselves are treated by the leaders of the companies for which they work, these leaders will be seen as pale reflections of Gordon Gecko—sleek, lazy lizards warming themselves in the hot sun, waiting with a snake-like tongue to ensnare a hapless fly.

PLAYING
TO WIN

IV

I don't want to find myself in a nursing home someday, thinking that all I did was play it safe.

THE TITLE OF this chapter is a tribute to my friend and mentor, Larry Wilson. Larry is the founder of Wilson Learning, a company which he sold in the mid-80's. He is currently President, CEO and founder of Pecos River Learning Center, based in Minneapolis, Minnesota.

Larry is the master teacher on the subject of employee training and team building. His company name evolved from a ranch (which he has now sold) in Santa Fe, New Mexico, located on the Pecos River.

In early 1992, I visited the ranch along with 35 of my key business associates. We attended a three-day session entitled "Play to Win." This experience changed my life.

At Pecos, I learned to "Taste Life." This acronym means:

• *Trust* • *Accountability* • *Support* • *Truth* • *Energy*

The key letter from the word "Taste" that left a lasting impression on me was the "S" for Support. The more I learn about how people interact, the more I realize the importance of giving teammates total support. Strong emotional support is absolutely essential to "ferocious cooperation." Without emotional support for your team, you will have bickering, politicking and bureaucracy.

Playing to Win is about "going as far as you can with all you have." Fear is what causes most people to "play not to lose." It is natural to avoid anything that brings us pain. When we "play not to lose," we avoid pain and fear and keep doing the same things over and over. This keeps us in a comfort zone. Playing to Win is about moving outside the comfort zone, and stretching to win. Any stretch is a win.

I guess there's a point in everyone's life where he or she decides whether to go through life and see what happens, or to truly go for it. It's hard to "play to win" if, in fact, you don't believe it's possible. Restated, it may be hard to see yourself as successful and making a difference unless you really believe you can. First you must believe in you.

I think it first dawned on me that I would be more than average the summer after my freshman year in college. I had made up my mind I was going to pay for the balance of my expenses. After my freshman year at Oklahoma State University, I took a summer job with the Southwestern Company, based in Nashville, Tennessee. I had no idea what I was about to get into, but being a fearless 18-year-old, I loaded my $1100 1966 Volkswagen and headed for Nashville, Tennessee, for a week's training.

The job entailed selling biblical books, door to door. The specific product I was trained to sell was called "The Layman's Bible Library," which consisted of an encyclopedia, a story book and a history book. I will never forget sitting in the training hall with over 1,000 college kids. I listened to several people make presentations, which I thought were pretty bad. I can remember continuing to say to myself, "If these people can sell, I am going to be rich."

We graduated from the training, and I headed to Middletown, Ohio, in my Volkswagen to sell "The Layman's Bible Library." The set of books was priced at $27.95. My take per set was $13.50, so the way I had it figured, if I could sell two sets a day, seven days a week for ten weeks, I had a pretty good shot of making $2,000 for the summer. This would be more than enough money to pay for my entire sophomore year.

I grew up in a fairly affluent family. My father was a dentist, so I had the belief that people who would buy these books would come from affluent neighborhoods; and that's exactly where I headed for my first sales calls. As you might expect, I learned early on that this was the hardest group of people to sell. The rich didn't like a book salesman knocking on their door. They were too busy, and if nothing else, were probably afraid to open the door. In fact, I found my success in the low- to middle-income neighborhoods because these people better understood the pain I was going through, randomly knocking on doors. I can assure you, it was painful. It was the most difficult job I ever had. You can't believe how many different ways people can say "No."

There was a period in early summer when I was about to give up, and then I rang the doorbell of the Heckerd residence. An attractive girl named Kathy, who was my age, answered. She had just finished her freshman year at Purdue. Her family invited me in, and she and I struck up a friendship for the balance of the summer. Her father was an executive with Armco Steel. He recommended that I discontinue selling my books and offered to help me get a job at Armco.

I refused to give up my book sales; so during the last few weeks of the summer, I worked approximately 40 hours a week at Armco Steel and 30 - 40 hours a week selling my books. Between the two jobs, I managed to come home with over $3,000, after expenses. I did this because I believed I would.

During my summer in Ohio, I remember continually thinking about the fear of failure as I received daily rejection in my door-to-door sales calls. I guess this is what caused me to take the second job, so I could be sure I didn't fail. The result was a double win for me, even though I must admit I never reached the goals I had set for myself as a door-to-door salesman. But it was okay, because I had far exceeded my financial goals for the summer and had some fun in the process.

When I returned to OSU to begin my sophomore year, I really felt good about myself and believed, for sure, that I would be successful in life. I remember the looks of respect on my fraternity brothers' faces, because they knew I had given up a summer of potential play to push myself outside the comfort zone which altered the entire course of my life.

What I remember most was coming home from that long summer with a "wad" of money and knowing I had pushed myself further than I ever dreamed that I could. I decided that I was going to take risks throughout my life and stretch myself to be more than average. I knew that if I could sell religious books, door to door, I could probably sell anything.

My experience in Ohio for the summer turned out to be just the beginning of a series of jobs that I had throughout college, which included being a houseboy at three different sorority houses, a teacher's assistant, working for A. C. Nielsen running a student placement survey that lasted almost two years, drawing beer and waiting tables at the local hamburger pub. I realize now that each job taught me something about people. Learning about people and how people feel about themselves is the most important learning a leader can get.

When I graduated from Oklahoma State University in 1971, I had paid the majority of all costs associated with my education. I knew I was responsible for my own well-being, and in fact, my life would be a series of games in which I would "play to win."

The funny part about the events of the summer of '68 is that I could have lived at home, helped my fraternity brothers with rush, had a regular, low-stress summer job and lived it up. But I was determined to make it on my own. I guess I was trying to prove something. I still am. I like taking calculated risks and love "going as far as I can with all I have." I don't want to find myself in a nursing home someday, thinking that all I did in life was play it safe.

WALKING
YOUR
TALK

V

There was no way I was going to ask people to climb a pole or scale a wall without doing it with them.

IT SEEMS LIKE every time I pick up a book related to people in business, I read about how organizations are changing around the world. Invariably, a key word that surfaces is "empowerment." We are all familiar with the military model that has been employed in organizations for thousands of years. While most of us would agree that this military model has value to show who reports to whom, the reality of it is, we all report to the results or the outcome of the game that we're playing.

We all have clients to please; and if we exceed their expectations as we provide our products and services, we will win. The question is, "How should today's organization function to meet these goals?" Many CEO's, who are in their mid-fifties or sixties, grew up before we even had a business definition for the word "empowerment." There is clearly a struggle taking place in the business world from this group, who have great difficulty letting go of their command and control to a younger generation who see the value of "empowerment" of organizations.

In the companies I have helped turn around, it has become clear to me that the easiest way to be successful is to find or grow outstanding people and teach them a corporate culture which supports them in finding and growing other outstanding people. A leader's job is to set the vision and values of the organization and then seek mutually agreeable buy-in for what the organization is trying to become. This requires empowerment and trust; but in order to feel good about empowering people, a leader must be committed to total excellence as it relates to the quality of the people and their values. More specifically, an empowerment program won't work unless each individual is prepared to "Walk his/her own Talk." This means your words and your behavior match.

When I arrived at Interface Americas, one of the first things I did was to remove the private parking places for the executives. This simple decision caused quite a stir; but it sent a strong signal that top management, in fact, puts their pants on the same way as everyone else, regardless of the difference in pay levels and authority.

In January, 1992, I attended a Young Presidents' Organization university in Maui, Hawaii, and had the opportunity to hear Robert Galvin, the Chairman of Motorola, speak. I believe Motorola is one of the finest corporations in the world. They are a Six Sigma, first quality company. As importantly, Motorola is known for how they treat their people. Motorola believes in extensive training and feels that every associate should "own his or her job."

Someone from the audience asked Robert Galvin the question "How do you decide how and whom to promote from within your company?" His answer was simple and powerful. He said, "We only ask one question when trying to decide among qualified candidates, and it is, 'Is he or she a role model?'" Role models don't send mixed messages between what they say and how they behave. Boss-watching is still a hobby in most companies. However, over time and as organizational structures change, boss-watching may diminish as the boss becomes a leader. True leaders spend their energies nurturing other leaders.

Lee Iacocca believes there are only two important things a CEO should worry about — hiring and training good people and setting the right priorities.

In going through Larry Wilson's "Play to Win" and "Let Go" (Leading Empowered Teams to Grow) programs, I have learned the power of "Walking your Talk." We built a ropes course on site, at our business and ran two-day "Play to Win" sessions with every employee involved (17 sessions to be exact). I participated in virtually all events. There was no way I was going to ask people to climb a pole or scale a wall without doing it with them. On the surface, this may sound like I was wasting my time; not so, and that's the lesson most of today's managers do not understand.

My friends at Pecos River Learning Center provide the best vehicle I know of to break loose and realign business cultures, but it only works 100% if the boss becomes a leader. This means climbing the wall with everyone.

The power of the Pecos experience is best told through my friend, Ruth Souther. At the time we entered into the Pecos program, Ruth was over 60 years of age and had been with the company over 30 years. She was told by her doctor that she could not take part in the outdoor events because of high blood pressure. Ruth was determined she was, in fact, going to participate. She began to exercise and diet with discipline. She lost weight and gained strength. It was not long before Ruth's blood pressure came down and her doctor gave her permission to participate.

One of the key outdoor events required each associate to climb a 25′ pole, while being belayed (supported by emergency lines) by teammates. Everyone was asked to go as far as he or she could, and to "push themselves outside their comfort zone." I was on the belay line that day when Ruth came over to me and hugged me before she made her way to the pole. She was scared to death, and her hands were shaking as she clung to me.

She looked up, grabbed the ladder, and one step at a time, she made her way to the 12″ round platform (about the size of a small pizza) atop the pole. As she grasped the round disk and made her last step to the top, my heart almost jumped out of my chest for joy and love. I yelled at her to center herself, and someone else urged her to stop, breathe and observe. We were all proud, but no one more so than I. Ruth is a special person and someone I will never forget. Seeing that gallant woman stand on top of that pole with victory on her face moved us all.

If I had elected to do the first group only, then I would have missed the Ruth Souther victory. And Ruth would have missed me. True leaders cannot be absent from the action. When they are, the troops can crumble. They might grumble: "I bet he's sitting in some soft leather chair while I'm busting my fanny climbing this ridiculous pole. What the heck is this all about anyway?"

No one who saw my fanny go up the pole could ask this question, now could they?

BUILDING
YOUR
TEAM

VI

*If leaders can create a culture
and a team with frequently
shared values that are focused
on a mission, no one can stop
them from being successful.*

MY COLLEGE YEARS were great for a lot of reasons, mainly
because of my fraternity. I suppose the Greek society is a little
different at every college and university. Each campus offers
differing degrees of importance for fraternal life. At
Oklahoma State, the Greek system is strong and I had the
opportunity to be a member of what was then, and I still
believe to be, the best fraternity on campus.

As freshmen pledges, we lived in the house in conditions
very similar to a military environment during our pledgeship.
This period lasted from early September until mid-March.
There was no physical hazing; however, the members had one
clear mission, and that was to get the pledges to jell as a team
as soon as possible. This is no easy task. Thirty-five individuals from all walks of life are, all of a sudden, put in a house
and told, "Become one."

I was initiated into Sigma Nu March 13, 1968, after six

months of hard work and team building with my 34 pledge brothers. I regard becoming a Sigma Nu as one of my best personal accomplishments. It was because the experience taught me first hand how leadership affects the group.

It has only been recently that I have realized the importance of the connection between my fraternity life and what I have been doing in business for the last 24 years. If leaders can create a culture and a team with frequently shared values that are focused on a mission, no one can stop them from being successful. This in no way suggests diminishing the importance of individuality or diversity as critical to team success, because great teams need both. Most companies don't even know for sure why they're in business. This is why organizations are now writing mission statements — to signal what they stand for and are trying to become. Mission statements are great if they really say what you mean and if you do what you say.

The creed of Sigma Nu is:
"To believe in the life of love"
"To walk in the way of honor"
"To serve in the light of truth"
"This is the life, the way and the light of Sigma Nu."
"This is the creed of our fraternity."

This creed is the mission and vision of Sigma Nu. I now know the importance of organizations defining what they are trying to become. If you don't know, who does? This is why vision is important and why companies are now writing vision statements.

Our friends at Pecos River Learning Center believe that

the best vision is to get your team to create a company that, if it existed, would put you out of business. Most people spend more time planning their vacations than they do their lives, and most companies are more worried about the current quarter or year than what their real mission and vision is in business. Leaders need vision, but they must have a team connected at the hip to then create the organizational mission. This will be best accomplished by looking forward two to four years and envisioning what the company could look like in a perfect world. In order to create change and take this kind of risk, we need incredible support teams. So what organizations need is a mutually agreed upon set of reasons as to why they are going to connect as individuals, form a team and make a difference in their personal and professional lives.

What I'm talking about is very emotional. While this emotionalism might be scary to left-brains, it truly constitutes what I believe is my personal secret for success.

As a Sigma Nu pledge, I will never forget the infamous "Black Monday." This was when the "member pledge line was set." This meant from that point forward, the pledge class had to sink or swim as a team. The goal of every pledge class is to get initiated as soon as possible. This ends the misery of pledging. There are powerful parallels in life to the six-month pledgeship. What I now know is that we really live our lives in one continuous pledgeship. Larry Wilson would say, "We live in continuous white water." There is really no place to hide from today's competitive environment. This is why it is vital for teams to be emotionally connected in order to survive. If we believe in ourselves and we believe in our teammates, we have almost all the belief we need to face the perils of our daily lives. The rest of the belief is, of course, in God. Without God, you cannot get out of bed.

As Sigma Nu pledges, we were charged to do a once-a-week thorough housecleaning. We called it "white-gloving." This event started at 1:00 am Saturday morning and concluded when the house was perfect. If any member could find dirt anywhere, we had to start over again. This is an interesting parallel to the continuous improvement quality process in business. After a few weeks, we learned the game and cut our housecleaning time from six hours to two hours. It's amazing how you learn to change the game when you want to sleep.

The members wanted the pledges to operate with a philosophy of "We are going on a journey. We will carry the wounded and shoot the stragglers."

Today, many of my closest friends are my fraternity brothers. We are bound by the trauma of the experiences we shared as young men. As I look back, these were some of the best years of my life. That's why I continuously seek to recreate the team of Sigma Nu.

I want people around me whom I love and who love me in return. I will demonstrate my trust in you, my commitment to you, and how deeply I care about you — in short, I will suffer for you. If you will demonstrate your trust in me, your commitment to me, and how deeply you care about me — in short, if you will suffer for me, then and only then can we play on the same team. Because then we will be unbeatable.

HELPING
OTHERS

VII

It takes no effort at all to tell your employees, 'I care about you'.

IN JULY, 1992, our family attended a Young Presidents' Organization family outing at Amelia Island, Florida. Little did I know that this trip would end up having a significant, long-term, positive impact on our family and the lives of many associates in the two organizations where I have worked since that time. This is where I met my close friend, Dr. J. Zink. J. is a family therapist who lives in Manhattan Beach, California. He has written five books, *Building Positive Self-Concept in Kids*; *Motivating Kids*; *Ego States*; *Dearly Beloved: The Secrets of Successful Marriage*; and *The Parent Your Parents Were Not*. You would do well to read them.

YPO is a worldwide organization encompassing approximately 8,000 members. I'm told that if it was a country, it would enjoy the sixth largest gross national product in the world. Needless to say, this is a powerful group. All YPO consultants are rated after each presentation. Dr. J. Zink is the highest rated YPO resource in the world. So he knows how to connect emotionally with his audience. J. could work anywhere he wanted.

When I first met Dr. J. that summer, he was struggling to keep his wife, Kern, alive. Kern had been a diabetic since she was 16 years of age. As Kern's health failed, J. and his son, Joe, were caring for Kern at home. During this time, J.'s personal net worth diminished to the point that collectors were harassing him to pay hospital bills. Kern Zink passed away on November 24, 1993.

I joined Interface Americas November 9, 1993. In January 1994, in conjunction with my new assignment, J. and I hooked up on a mission that has become unique and almost revolutionary in American business. I decided to provide J. as a resource to all our associates, regardless of pay or position. This meant that any Interface employee could speak with J. by telephone, and in many cases, in person.

J. came to LaGrange, Georgia, one week a month, and counseled our employees on family problems. Up front, J. and I agreed on a "Chinese Wall," which meant that I did not want to know any information concerning any discussions he had with any associate.

When I joined Interface Americas, things looked bleak; morale was low, our sales and margins were declining. I knew it was important that our new leadership team do everything possible to capture the emotional capital of the company. I knew this could be accomplished by helping people work through their personal and professional pain. Since that time, our company has provided Dr. J. Zink as a speaker to several churches in our community, to our customers and even to friends of our employees.

J. and I really never established many rules except that we were on a mission to do what was right. We actually made the rules as we worked our way through this new approach to "helping others." I think Interface history will show this approach was, in fact, revolutionary.

As J. and I got to know each other better, he became my mentor and motivator. I really can't tell stories about J.'s success at Interface, because I don't know the stories. I do know that he was very busy his first few months; and now, he has more time to work on the pro-active, positive things that we can do to create the best company in the world. We invested money and faith in Dr. J. Zink and got back more than money can buy.

Most people will agree, we're all moving at lightning speed in our daily lives, and the pressure to perform and produce results is taxing our physical and mental capabilities. This takes its toll on our families. It's so important to remember that we all have a breaking point and that we need help and support with life's challenges.

Retaining the services of Dr. J. Zink was the best business decision of my career, because I have been a recipient of the joy of helping others through their own pain. While I don't know the details, I get notes, hugs and thank-you's because of J., on a regular basis.

Management which fails to recognize that the reason people come to work in the first place is to provide for their families is short-sighted, self-serving management. This type of management fails at the most basic level of the human experience. This management forgets why we are all here.

It takes no effort at all to tell your employees "I care

about you." But providing them the services of one of the finest family therapists in the world at no cost to them showed them that our company cares.

That, as Robert Frost says, has made all the difference.

TAKING
CARE OF
YOURSELF

VIII

We need to assume other people are watching us and as importantly, watch out for ourselves.

DURING MY CAREER, I have often been kidded about the fact that I take time off. As a matter of fact, I'm writing this specific chapter as I sit in the sun in Bermuda. I have, in fact, taken my fair share of vacations, almost always with my family; however, if you talk to my family, they will tell you their number one job was to keep me off the telephone. I'll never forget the summer of '93, when we went to Santa Fe, New Mexico, and I made a commitment to my family that I wouldn't call in for the entire week. I made it until Thursday, which was a big accomplishment for me.

While on vacation, I am usually reading, writing and planning my week, month, year and career. In almost every case, I return full of life and new energy concerning the task and opportunities that lie ahead.

More importantly, these trips have given our family time to enjoy each other, reflect and just have fun. I deeply believe that my happiness and health is a direct result of blending time off with the fast pace of life that I live.

Over the years, I've known many associates who seemed to enjoy bragging about the fact that they hadn't had a vacation in years. This is a bad choice. Taking care of one's health is a continual challenge because of all the temptation in the world to eat and drink the wrong things. We have to work at it and do our best to discipline ourselves. As grandfather Eitel said, "anything to excess is bad."

My wife, Cindy, had an uncle who lived to be 96. He claimed that the key to his good health was the eight glasses of water he drank every day. I've been trying to imitate Uncle Pete for years and I, in fact, drink about eight glasses of bottled water a day.

The right diet and exercise are essential to achieve a balanced life. It's just a matter of forming the right habits. Believe me, I'm not trying to preach and am far from achieving my own health goals; but in our hearts, we all know we must take care of our health.

Our family tries to spend at least one week a year snow skiing and one week scuba diving. It makes sense to blend vacations with sports activities. I call it a true "win, win!" All families must take care not to promote destructive competition among the children. The same team building rules for business teams work for family teams as well. Support, support, support!

The rule at Pecos is simple: No zingers! Zingers are comments which hurt. Zingers are often said to be funny. But laughing at someone else's expense is not funny.

By taking care of yourself, you are also taking care of others. After all, we all have people depending on us. Even if you don't particularly care about your health, I can assure you others do, particularly your family. It only takes 21 days to form habits; why not make them good?

Before Kern Zink died, she asked Dr. J. to make three promises, which were:

- *Eat right*
- *Exercise*
- *Help others*

This is what J. calls "The Wisdom of Kern." J. says that Kern believed that by eating right, exercising and helping others, we build a pathway to God. I sure agree with that!

You may notice that the majority of this book has focused on the period of my career from 1981 to 1994. I actually got involved in the floorcoverings industry as my first job fresh out of college. My friend and mentor, Bud Seretean, founder of Coronet Carpets, offered me a position as a management trainee, during his visit to our mutual alma mater, Oklahoma State University.

My ten years at Coronet were a tremendous education. If Bud had stayed at the helm, I probably would have never left. I have a tremendous amount of respect for Bud for a lot of reasons too lengthy to mention; but for sure, I owe him for my first big business break in life. Thanks, Bud!

As a young 21-year-old college graduate, you tend to pay close attention to the top management of a company. Back then, Bud Seretean seemed like a king. This fact often reminds me that I have to "walk my own talk."

When it comes to taking care of yourself, Bud sets the best example of anyone I know. He is 70 years of age and looks and acts like he is 20 years younger. In the last decade, he has dedicated a great deal of his time and money to educate our youth on wellness and fitness. Bud is the major donor for The Seretean Center for Health Promotion now under construction at Emory University in Atlanta, Georgia. He also provided the primary funds for The Oklahoma State University Wellness Center in Stillwater, Oklahoma.

When Bud speaks to groups, he focuses on the importance of developing six points to develop the right lifestyle. These six points are:

- *Exercise*
- *Diet*
- *Weight control*
- *Stress control*
- *Substance abuse control (liquor, smoking, drugs)*
- *Accident prevention*

Teaching people how to eat is difficult, because unlike smoking or drinking problems, we cannot stop eating. Our bodies need certain balanced nutrition. That is all they need. I think that most people overeat because they are starved for affection and support. Confusing the need for affection with the need for food could make you one fat cookie.

In the final analysis, taking care of yourself means learning how to be your own best friend. Think about it: Your best friend doesn't criticize or judge you. Your best friend listens to what you have to say. Your best friend supports you emotionally and yells positive things that make a lot of sense when you succeed. Your best friend says, when you fail, "Hey, forget it. You'll get 'em next time. Just wait 'til they see you next year, pal."

We need to assume other people are watching us and as importantly, watch out for ourselves.

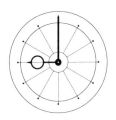

HAVING
FUN

IX

*Make sure your mission is for you
and not for your parents.*

IT SEEMS THAT almost everyone would agree they would like to think of themselves as being successful in life, both professionally and personally. The word "successful" is generic. It can mean something different to everyone.

This thought reminds me of a speech I made to a group of young people a few years ago at my alma mater, Oklahoma State University. I had very little time to prepare my presentation, so all I could do was stop and reflect on what I thought would be the most important things to tell these young students. I wanted to help perpetuate their successes.

I began my own college career thinking I was going to be a dentist. I suppose this was true because this was my father's profession. Early on, I knew I was in trouble because I hated chemistry; and my grades reflected my dislike for the subject. During my sophomore year, I realized I did not want to be a dentist. It may have been a form of subconscious rebellion, even though my father said he did not want me to be a dentist. Powerful sons of powerful fathers have to rebel in some way. Otherwise, they could never stand up to life's challenges on their own. (I will have to remember I wrote that when my powerful son rebels from me.)

It was during my sophomore year in college that the clouds finally parted, and I began to realize that the key to success and happiness is to do what makes you happy. I realized I needed to try to figure out how to have fun and also make a living. As a 19-year-old, I never realized I would end up focusing my career in the floorcoverings industry. However, what I did realize is that I enjoyed helping to lead and develop other people.

So, when I spoke to the group of students at OSU, what I told them was simply this: "The key to being successful is to be happy; and in order to be happy, you need to be spending your time doing what makes you happy and gives you a sense of accomplishment. You have to listen for a while to learn what your life's mission will be. We all have one. Make sure your mission is for you and not for your parents."

Even though I've always been in the field of making a product, specifically "carpet," I focus on the people side of business more than the product side. When it all comes down to it, I think it's important that we all feel we've made a significant contribution or left something behind that will be remembered.

After my speech to the students, I had a question from a young lady in the audience. She said that all she liked to do was ride horses, but she couldn't imagine how she could make a living at it. I suggested she might try selling saddles for a living. She smiled at that.

The famed business author Peter Drucker was recently asked what career path he would recommend for his grandchildren in this fast-changing world. He said, "Figure out what you are good at and become excellent at it."

Some managers think that having fun requires a competitive activity. As I get older, I realize that it is more important to teach people how to compete fairly in this wonderful free enterprise system and how to cooperate with each other, in the best interest of our customers. If you really stop and think about it, how many people do you know who are so intent on winning in sports that they really miss the entire point? The journey of life is the fun. It's not what you've done or what you're going to do, but it is what you are doing right now that matters.

When I play golf, I do so mainly because I enjoy being outside. I enjoy the weather and fellowship. If I hit a bad shot (which I often do), I try not to get mad because doing so would cause me to get upset about something that's not that important. Obviously, this is not totally true for the professional golfer. However, if you really study the best golfers in the world, you will find that they do a remarkable job of keeping cool and staying focused on the repeatable process they've developed and mastered over the years. As my friend Doug Garwood will tell you, "90% of the success of a golf shot is setting it up correctly. Then pull the trigger."

Most people know golf is not an easy game. Neither is life a bed of roses; quite the opposite. Life's satisfactions come from these very challenges, not material possessions.

Some of the happiest people I've met have been at the various islands such as the Caymans and Bermuda. They have simply decided the price they were having to pay to do what made them unhappy wasn't worth the material things; therefore, they said "to heck with it" and are now doing what makes them happy, which can be something as simple as driving a cab or being an outdoor guide. I guess this always amazes me in that these are some of the bravest people in the world. They seemed to have concluded that life's needs are more important than life's wants. If you cannot say that you are as happy as you have the potential to be, I recommend you take action. The alternative choice may cost you your life.

After one's God, there are three big games in life:
- *Being a husband/wife*
- *Being a parent*
- *Having a profession*

If the time you spend on all three is in balance, then you have a much greater chance of being happy. If you are failing in one or more of these roles, then you need to get busy. As Grandfather Eitel would have said, "Daylight's burning, son."

BEING
ACCOUNTABLE

X

The payback may be long or never.
The key point here is that we have
made decisions about values that
are driving this mission.

KEN BLANCHARD AND Norman Vincent Peale wrote a book, *The Power of Ethical Management*. In this book, they cite a method to check with your conscience as to whether the decision you are about to make is right or wrong. It's simply this, "Would you be proud to see your actions from this decision published on the front page of your local newspaper?"

At Interface, we are committed to being accountable for our actions. This way of life goes far beyond the requirements of being a public company.

We are particularly sensitive to every environmental issue. We are striving to achieve a goal of zero waste. Effective January 1, 1995, we have a launched a worldwide "War on Waste," using a zero-based waste philosophy. We have named this life change "Quest to Deliver Superior Value." Quest stands for Quality Using Employee Suggestions and Teamwork.

The best way to build world class products or services is to design them "Right the First Time." Being accountable for the products you design is a very misunderstood strategy for most companies.

At Interface, our product meetings are the lifeblood of everything we do. These meetings include people from all disciplines of the company so we can be sure we are communicating on quality, costs, equipment, capacity, service, human resources, and of equal importance, environmental issues. We are committed to giving our customers more with less. We believe, in many cases, "less is actually more."

We are striving to perfect a "cradle to cradle" way of life, and have developed what we call our "Account/Ability circle." It is best understood to read it clockwise in that it represents the order of events in which we believe products and processes are developed. You will note that the words "Account/Ability" are in the center of the circle, which is a metaphor for the customer being in the center of all for which we stand. As you review this "Account/Ability" circle, you will note that everything starts with values.

You can have all the technology and money in the world, but if you try to run your business without the right basic values, you will fail. This is why I have devoted the majority of this book to this belief.

Interface is the world's largest manufacturer of carpet tile (squares) and specified contract carpet. Our principal raw material is nylon. Nylon is made from petrochemicals, which we know are a finite reserve. Our company is committed to doing everything in our power to return our product to our product in an "Eco Sense" or "Cradle to Cradle" mentality. This means we will take back what we sell our customers, recycle it, and sell it again. Our goal is to recycle everything.

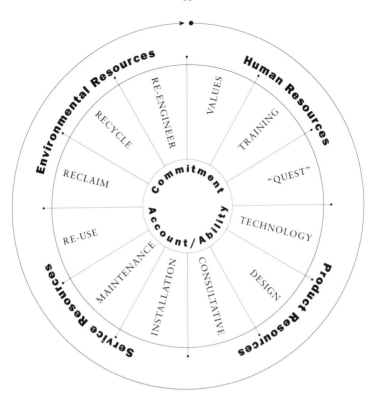

It is the right thing to do.

Being environmentally conscious is a tall order because much like our GED program, the payback may be long or never. The key point here is that we have made decisions about values that are driving this mission. Our chairman, Ray Anderson, has launched our "Eco Sense" world mission. He, along with all our associates, are doing everything possible to "walk the talk." It is a timeless, endless mission, and one which truly must be passed on to the next generations with increasing commitment.

In my "Account/Ability" circle, you will note that "reengineer" is the last thing we do to close the loop on a "Cradle to Cradle" mission.

In 1993, I met Bill McDonough, who is the owner of an architectural firm in New York. Bill is now Dean of the School of Architecture at the University of Virginia. He gave me a quote I will never forget: "Waste = Food." This fact has changed the entire way I look at non-value added processes and the abuse of materials. Bill's point is that we should not accept the word waste into our vocabulary, but rather force ourselves to close our food chain (food to food).

In 1994, I had the pleasure to meet yet another unique person, John Picard, who has further elevated our company's focus on eliminating waste and environmental abuse. John is the owner of the firm E² Environmental Enterprises, Inc., based in California. John is effecting dramatic change on our environmental mission at Interface. He pushes and challenges us almost daily.

We need more people like Bill McDonough and John Picard, who are obsessed with saving Planet Earth.

I suppose anyone can draw his/her own "Account/Ability" circle, and that it can mean different things to different people. The point here is simple: We are going to leave the ecology of the earth better than we found it.

As the saying goes, "If you don't stand for something, you will fall for anything." The time for profit at the expense of the planet has passed. This is where we stand.

At Interface, we approach our customers by acting as

consultants. We ask them to trust us and if they are not happy with our advice or products, they don't pay. This simple, bottom-line approach to being accountable has welcomed our customers into our culture of "ferocious cooperation."

In this day and age, there is simply too much to know about too many things. With corporate downsizing, most companies simply do not have the resources to analyze all the facts they would like to, so they must make decisions, based on trust. Much like the Bible, one's belief is based on fact as far as it can be understood, and faith and trust must carry us the rest of the way.

My friend, Larry Wilson, has a new book, *Stop Selling and Start Partnering*. I highly recommend it as a textbook which examines the future of the buyer/seller relationship. Larry's concept of partnering opens the door to creating this feeling I am calling "ferocious cooperation." The fight here is not with each other; it is for each other. Interface associates are fighting to get our clients the best possible value. Our intent is to hold their long-term best interests above our short-term gains and become good friends and co-conspirators in the pursuit of excellence.

At Interface, we ask our associates to ask themselves "What am I being paid to do?" It's a real gut check. Peter Drucker believes that the key issue is to try and figure out how to get all associates of an organization to be responsible and accountable for their actions. In all organizations, there are four groups that know what is right and wrong. Those making, counting, selling and buying your products or services. Just listen!

REFLECTING
TIME

XI

Do you ever stop and ask yourself,
'how did I get here?'

DO YOU EVER stop and ask yourself, "How did I get here?" I do this all the time and thank the Lord for all my wonderful blessings. I also know that I am getting what I deserve, and so are you. At Pecos River Learning Center, Larry Wilson and his associates often ask participants in their programs, "What kind of results are you getting in your life?" The answer is, "You are getting what you should be getting because you are doing what you have been doing." Sounds simple, and it is. If you are not getting what you want, you may want to change something.

As I stop and reflect on my life, I am so thankful I met my one and only wife, Cindy, whom I love so very much. We have been married 24 years, and have the kind of relationship that most people would describe as perfect. Cindy is my true life partner. She is smart, sensitive and beautiful inside and out. This woman knows what I am thinking before I open my mouth. Cindy and the Lord are good friends. She keeps me focused on what is really important.

As a young executive coming up in the business world, I

often think of the choices I made between being with Cindy and the kids and that additional business meeting. I am fairly certain I could have been more successful financially if I had not put my family first. But I did and always will, and I still consider myself to have done well financially. After all, if I lost my family, I wouldn't have much of a life no matter how much money I had.

I recently had the opportunity to hear Lee Iacocca speak. He was asked the question, "If you could do it all over again, what would you change?" He said, "I would not have been so ambitious. I pushed too hard and it affected my health and family."

I would like to think that I have a pretty good size fan club from all my associations in business, and I guess the real test will come one of these days when I slow down. But I know for sure that if I end up in the intensive care unit some-day, Cindy, Jennifer, Stephanie and Chuck will be right there with me.

By now, I guess you have concluded we are a very close family. Since our children were small, we have employed a lady named Jessie Burditt. Jessie has had a very positive influence on our family in many dimensions. She has kept our physical house in order but more importantly, she has helped us keep our children on the right track. Jessie and her husband Elijah are very special.

I have had many bosses over the years; and as one might expect, I have had varying levels of respect for them. I am told that the number one reason people quit their jobs is because of the boss. I believe this is true. I am a living example.

The fun part about my story is that I have finally managed to end up working for a person I totally respect and trust. Ray Anderson is the founder of our company, Interface, Inc. We are a Fortune 500 company, with annual sales in excess of $700 million. We do business in over 110 countries.

Ray is honest, extremely hardworking, intelligent, simple in material possessions and loves his family and the company he founded. To Ray, Interface is a living, breathing being — his child!

For the first time in my life, I am working for someone I love. This fact makes me realize the importance of being a mentor, leader and "walking the talk." Ray Anderson is a remarkable person who is exceptionally kind-hearted. He is the kind of leader you want when the fast bullets fly. He is resourceful and perceptive. We work together as though we knew each other all of our lives. I am honored and proud to work for Ray.

Do your love your boss? Do you feel like your company is a family? If so, you have a competitive advantage. We spend too much time away from our natural families to be unhappy in our working family.

As I stop and reflect on my life, here is my personal list of thoughts that define who Charlie Eitel truly is:

- *My Davy Crockett coonskin hat*
- *My first saddle*
- *Feeding horses twice a day for years*
- *Growing up with four older sisters (Pat, Judy, Linda & Janet)*
- *Being a baseball catcher for eight years*

- *Sitting on the bench in basketball more than I wanted*
- *The day I got initiated into Sigma Nu (March 13, 1968)*
- *My wedding day, May 22, 1971 (a little hung over)*
- *Our first home in Columbia, South Carolina*
- *The day our oldest daughter, Jennifer, was born on April 7, 1974 (the day before Hank Aaron hit number 715 over the fence)*
- *The day Jennifer flushed an apple, with one bite out of it, down the toilet*
- *The day Jennifer and I played in the baby pool*
- *The day Stephanie was born on November 19, 1976 (I almost did not make it home from a business trip.)*
- *The day Chuck was born on June 13, 1978 (my best man in our wedding , Dr. Gary Hill, was there. I must confess, the happiest day of my life)*
- *The "big wheels" in the driveway*
- *The yellow house*
- *The day I met and hired the world's best assistant, Linda Timms*
- *Jennifer playing the character "Annie" at the Little Theater*
- *Stephanie in her softball outfit*
- *Chuck's dinner prayer, "I've Been Working on the Railroad"*
- *Remembering the Christmas funnies inspired by Cindy's mother, Ila Fern McDougal*

- *Jennifer's senior singing recital in five languages*
- *Stephanie winning the Pentathlon*
- *Chuck's first football game*
- *Chuck's knee surgery (a success)*
- *The day I got stung by 17 fire ants*
- *The day I met Dr. J. Zink*
- *The day I met Larry Wilson*
- *The day I came to Interface*
- *The day I finished this book, December 31, 1994.*

Well, there you have it, reader. I have been as honest as I know how to be. Voltaire said, "Writing maketh an exact man." I now know what he meant.

I sure wish my fourth grade English teacher, who gave me a "C," were alive today to give me a better grade for my first book.

My true purpose in writing these words was to communicate not only with those who would read these values in my own time, but with future generations who will come to discover whether my ideas, as simple as they may be, will stand up to the test of time and the ideas of future generations.

Then, too, someday Jennifer or Stephanie or Chuck may have a baby on their knees and might say to the child, "Let me tell you about your grandpappy." Then I will be Grandfather Eitel!

PEACE
OF MIND

XII

What's the hurry?
Where are you going?

AS YOU THINK back on the eleven chapters you have read, hopefully you will notice there has been a logic in the order. If you think of this book as a clock, beginning at one o'clock, you will see the order much like the order of time.

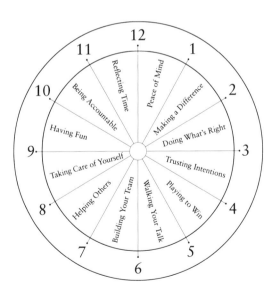

Eitel Time: Turnaround Secrets

Margaret Thatcher was recently asked what she hoped to accomplish during the rest of her life. She said, "To help countries come to democracy." According to John Naisbitt's new book, *The Global Paradox*, there are 302 countries in the world and cell dividing fast. Margaret Thatcher has a big job, but the fall of communism has helped pave the way. We as individuals need to bring democracy to ourselves by setting the right priorities and being accountable for our actions. We can all make a difference, but we must start with ourselves. Call it "The Power of One."

It is a lot easier to write and talk about the values in this book than to live them every day. Most of us end up doing what is natural because we are what we are. At the same time, I sincerely hope this short book has had a positive impact on how you live your life. If my work causes you to revisit just one of your own core values, I will have been a successful writer.

Behind my desk, I keep 14 quotations which I want to share with you. These words help keep the peace in my soul.

"THE FUTURE BELONGS TO THOSE WHO BELIEVE IN THE BEAUTY OF THEIR DREAMS."
Eleanor Roosevelt

"OBSTACLES ARE THOSE FRIGHTFUL THINGS YOU SEE WHEN YOU TAKE YOUR EYES OFF YOUR GOALS."
Unknown

"THE ONLY WAY I WILL KNOW THAT I HAVE REACHED MY LIMIT IS IF I PASS IT JUST ONCE."
Richie Harris

"WE ARE CONTINUALLY FACED BY GREAT
OPPORTUNITIES BRILLIANTLY DISGUISED AS
INSOLUBLE PROBLEMS."
Unknown

"DON'T TELL ME HOW HARD YOU WORK.
TELL ME HOW MUCH YOU GOT DONE."
James Ling

"ANYBODY CAN GET A POSITION THAT THEY CAN
GROW OUT OF. I HELP PEOPLE ATTAIN POSITIONS
THAT THEY CAN GROW INTO."
Richie Harris

"IT'S WHAT YOU LEARN AFTER YOU KNOW
IT ALL THAT COUNTS."
John Wooden

"CHARACTER IS THE ABILITY TO SAY, NO,
WHEN EVERYONE EXCEPT YOUR CONSCIENCE
IS SCREAMING, YES."
Richie Harris

"REAL LEADERS ARE ORDINARY PEOPLE WITH
EXTRAORDINARY DETERMINATION."
Unknown

"PEOPLE FORGET HOW FAST YOU DID A JOB — BUT
THEY REMEMBER HOW WELL YOU DID IT."
Howard W. Newton

"AS I GROW OLDER, I PAY LESS ATTENTION TO
WHAT MEN SAY — I JUST WATCH WHAT THEY DO."
Andrew Carnegie

"TO LOVE WHAT YOU DO AND FEEL THAT IT
MATTERS — HOW CAN ANYTHING BE MORE FUN?"
Katharine Graham

"A GREAT PLEASURE IN LIFE IS DOING WHAT
PEOPLE SAY YOU CANNOT DO."
Walter Gagehot

"SUCCESS IS A JOURNEY, NOT A DESTINATION."
Ben Sweetland

I will add the 15th quote:

"WHAT'S THE HURRY? WHERE ARE YOU GOING?"
Charlie Eitel

So, there you have it. Thanks for reading my book. J. D.
Salinger's famous character, Holden Caulfield, said that you
know you've read a good book if after you put it down you
want to call the author and chat. If this is the case for you,
my number is 404.437.6800; or you may write to me at
Interface, Inc., 2859 Paces Ferry Road, Suite 2000, Atlanta,
Georgia 30339. Let me hear from you.